YOUR PASSPORT TO
JAMAICA
by Golriz Golkar
CAPSTONE PRESS
a capstone imprint
I0820687

Published by Capstone Press, an imprint of Capstone
1710 Roe Crest Drive, North Mankato, Minnesota 56003
capstonepub.com

Library of Congress Cataloging-in-Publication Data is available on the Library of Congress website.
ISBN: 9798875245794 (hardcover)
ISBN: 9798875245749 (paperback)
ISBN: 9798875245756 (ebook PDF)

Summary: What is it like to live in or visit Jamaica? What makes Jamaica's culture unique? Explore the geography, traditions, and daily lives of Jamaicans.

Editorial Credits
Editor: Elaine Duncan; Designer: Sarah Bennett; Media Researcher: Rebekah Hubstenberger; Production Specialist: Tori Abraham

Image Credits
Alamy: Brian Gibbs, 9, Karol Kozlowski Premium RM Collection, 10, Ron Giling, 6; Capstone Press: Eric Gohl, 5; Getty Images: Fox Photos, 13, Holger Leue, 21, iStock/Didi Beck, 22, iStock/GummyBone, 16, iStock/sanniely, 17, Jed Jacobsohn, 26, Michael Ochs Archives, 14, Monty Rakusen, 20, Randy Brooks - CPL T20, 27; Shutterstock: BigMike Photos, cover, Divine Shot Multimedia, 15, Florida Chuck, 29, Griffin Gillespie, 19 (top), Lost Mountain Studio, 25, Peter Douglas Clark, 19 (bottom right), VIG-Vam, 18

Design Elements
Getty Images: iStock/Yevhenii Dubinko; Shutterstock: Flipser, Net Vector, petch one, pingebat, Suppawong Yaed

Printed and bound in Malaysia. 006460

CONTENTS

Words in **bold** are in the glossary.

CHAPTER ONE

WELCOME TO JAMAICA!

The sun rises over Fort Clarence Beach in Kingston, Jamaica. The turquoise waves of the Caribbean Sea splash along white, sandy beaches. Sea turtles nest in the sand. Some people sunbathe. Others swim and snorkel in the warm waters.

In the city, visitors stroll past colorful murals. They admire the historic buildings from Jamaica's past. The Devon House features the white columns of British Georgian architecture. It was once the home of one of the island's wealthiest residents, George Stiebel.

The scent of Jamaican jerk chicken and fried plantains lures people to the city's many cafés. Jamaica is a natural paradise with old traditions and a modern vibe.

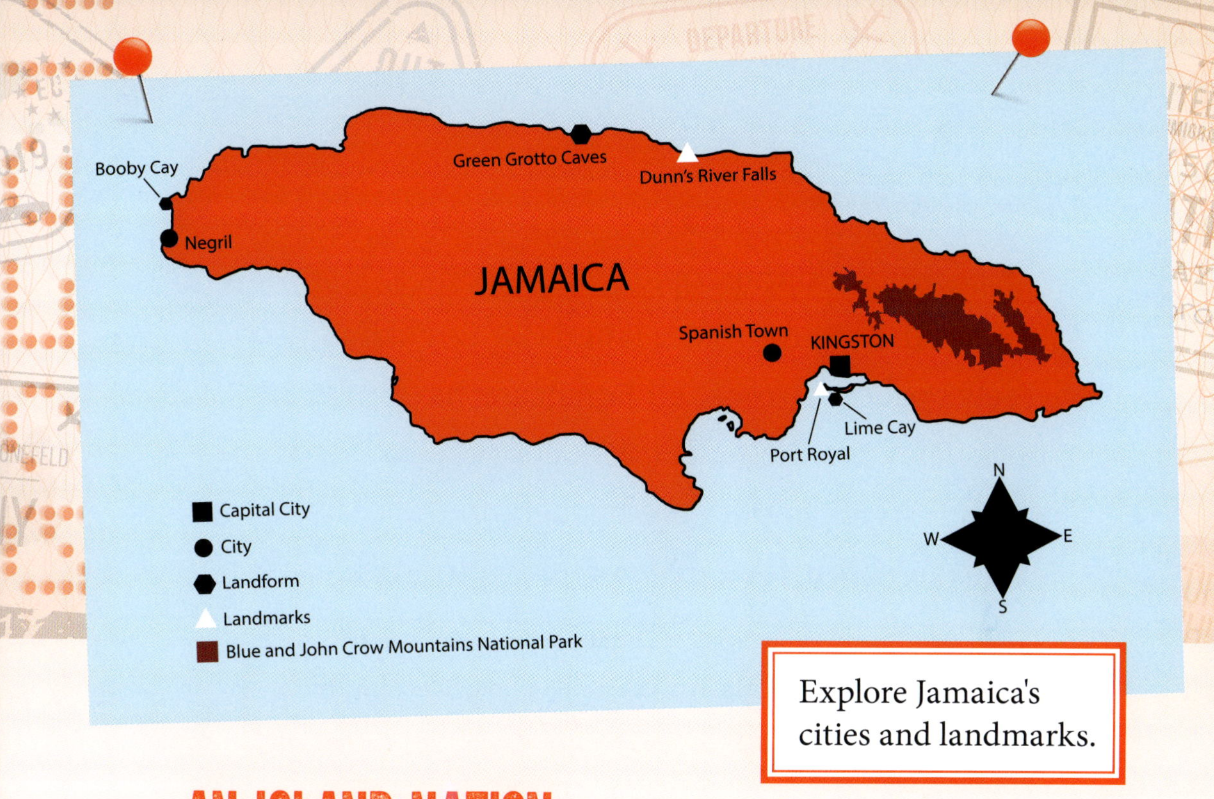

Explore Jamaica's cities and landmarks.

AN ISLAND NATION

Jamaica is an island country. It is surrounded by the Caribbean Sea. The country is part of the Greater Antilles islands northeast of Central America. Jamaica has a variety of landscapes. There are rainforests, rivers, and waterfalls. But it is mostly mountainous. Many sandy, low islands called cays rest on coral reefs surrounding the mainland.

Jamaica is **tropical**. Temperatures are warm year-round. Spring and fall are rainy seasons. The mountains receive the most rain. The southern coast is dry.

THE JAMAICAN PEOPLE

Nearly 3 million people live in Jamaica. Jamaican Patois is the main spoken language. English is also widely spoken. Almost all Jamaicans have African roots. They are the descendants of enslaved African people. These people were brought to the island by European **colonists** and were forced to work.

Children walk to school in Kingston, Jamaica.

FACT FILE

OFFICIAL NAME: .... JAMAICA

POPULATION: 2,837,956

LAND AREA: .... 4,243 SQ. MI. (10,992 SQ KM)

CAPITAL: .... KINGSTON

MONEY: .... JAMAICAN DOLLAR

GOVERNMENT: .... PARLIAMENTARY DEMOCRACY UNDER A CONSTITUTIONAL MONARCHY

LANGUAGE: .... JAMAICAN PATOIS AND ENGLISH

GEOGRAPHY: Jamaica is located in the Caribbean Sea. Haiti is to Jamaica's east. The Cayman Islands lie to the northwest. Cuba, to the north, is Jamaica's closest neighboring country.

NATURAL RESOURCES: sugar, bananas, aluminum, petroleum, coffee

FACT

Jamaica's national motto is "Out of Many, One People." It refers to how Jamaica is home to people of different backgrounds. But the Jamaican people consider themselves united as a common, proud people.

CHAPTER TWO

HISTORY OF JAMAICA

Indigenous people called the Taino first arrived in Jamaica around 600 CE. They came from South America. The Taino named the island Xaymaca. It means "land of wood and water." Many settled in villages near rivers to catch fish. They grew crops such as corn, cassava, and cotton. The Taino people created wood carvings, pottery, and rock art. They lived quietly in Jamaica for nearly 900 years.

THE EUROPEANS ARRIVE

Christopher Columbus was the first European to land in Jamaica in 1494. He claimed Jamaica for Spain. Spanish rulers used the island as a supply base. Horses, food, and equipment were shipped there to help the Spaniards **conquer** countries near North America. These Spaniards brought many African people.

The Spaniards fought the Taino for their land. Many Taino were killed, and others were enslaved. They were often forced to work on sugar plantations. Some died from being overworked. Others died from diseases brought by the Spanish. Within 50 years of the Spanish arrival, nearly all the Taino had been wiped out.

A reproduction of a Taino house made of wooden logs in Seville Heritage Park.

In 1509, the first Spanish colonists settled on the island. They founded the town of New Seville. Then in 1534 they moved the capital to what is now called Spanish Town. It became the center of government, trade, and religion. But management problems and little support from Spain weakened the colony.

In 1655, the British arrived and removed the Spaniards within five years. Many of the enslaved people escaped. They were called the Maroons. They formed their own free communities in the mountains.

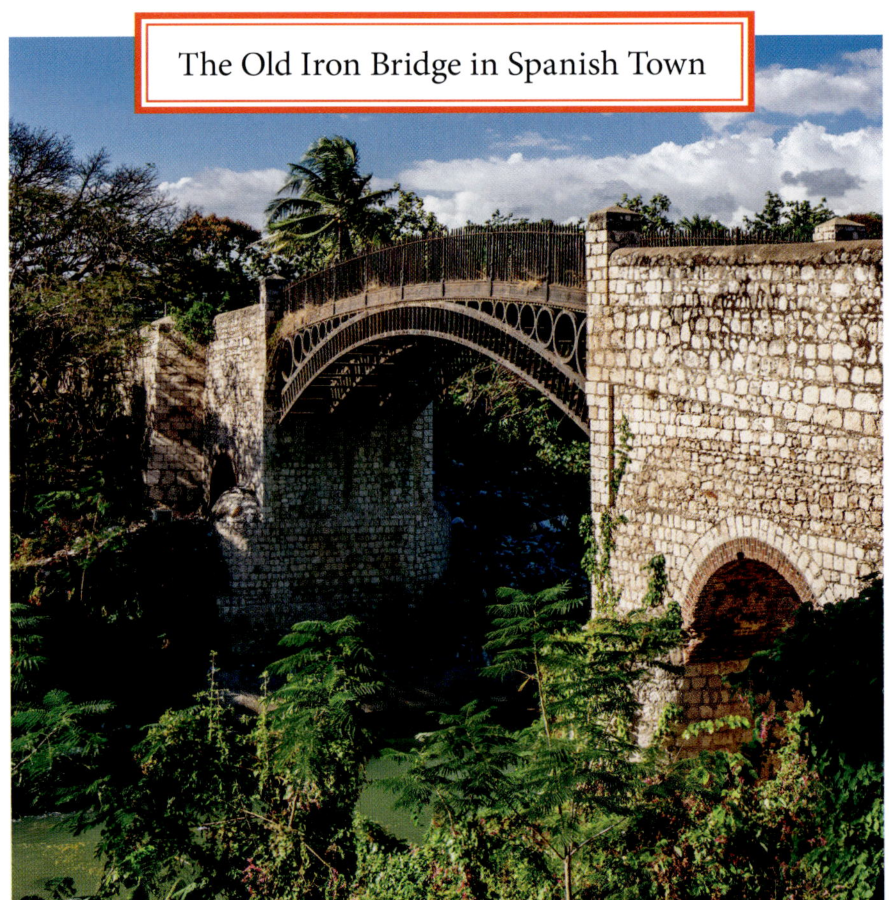
The Old Iron Bridge in Spanish Town

The British brought more enslaved people to the island. These people worked on plantations. Crops such as sugar, cacao, tobacco, and indigo were grown. By the 1680s, the population reached 18,000. But many enslaved people fought the British. Some escaped and joined the Maroons. Together, they formed small military groups and attacked the plantations. They set buildings on fire, stole guns, and fought bloody battles with plantation owners. The British finally gave in and signed a **treaty** in 1740. It gave the Maroons land and official freedom.

Over the next 100 years, some Christian groups spoke out against enslavement. They thought it was wrong to enslave people. Members of the British government were also afraid of more slave rebellions. In 1838, enslaved people were finally freed.

The plantation system ended since newly freed Jamaicans refused to work for former masters. The British Parliament changed the government of Jamaica to a crown colony system in 1866. A governor chosen by the British government held power over the island. Jamaica slowly became more modern. Schools, hospitals, and other public services improved.

MODERN JAMAICA

Starting in the mid-1800s, many **immigrants** came to Jamaica. They included large numbers of people from China, India, and the Middle East. Many of these immigrants became farmers and ran businesses. They strengthened Jamaica's **economy**. But in 1907, a strong earthquake and a fire damaged many cities. Many Jamaicans left the island to find work. The economy suffered.

Many people wanted a government that understood their concerns and **culture**. A new constitution was written in 1944 with a new government in place. It allowed all adults to vote, limited government power, and recognized political parties. In 1962, Jamaica became an independent nation. The island remains a member of the British Commonwealth, keeping friendly ties with the United Kingdom.

FACT

The Taino language has died out, but many of its words are still spoken. Taino words include "canoe," "hurricane," "hammock," and "barbeque."

TIMELINE OF JAMAICAN HISTORY

ABOUT 600 CE: The Taino arrive in Jamaica.

1494: Christopher Columbus claims Jamaica for Spain.

1510: Spanish colonists arrive and bring Africans to work on plantations as enslaved people.

1655: The British take Jamaica from Spain.

1838: Enslaved people are set free in Jamaica.

1866: Jamaica becomes a crown colony.

1938: Jamaicans riot against unemployment and unfair racial policies.

1944: A new constitution gives adults voting rights and the first elections are held for local governments.

1962: Jamaica becomes an independent nation within the British Commonwealth.

1976: Rival political parties cause violence in the streets before a major election.

2006: Portia Simpson Miller becomes Jamaica's first female prime minister.

2016: Jamaica wins 11 summer Olympic medals in athletics events.

Jamaican people celebrate Independence Day on August 6.

CHAPTER THREE

EXPLORE JAMAICA

Jamaica is an island paradise with many natural wonders and historic attractions. Visitors can discover the island's lush landscapes and rich culture.

MODERN CITIES

Kingston is the capital of Jamaica. Visitors can buy colorful handmade goods at the Kingston Craft Market. A tour of the Bob Marley Museum looks into the life of the world-famous Jamaican musician. The botanical gardens showcase many native plants and flowers.

THE MUSIC OF BOB MARLEY

Bob Marley was a famous reggae musician. His music spoke of peace, love, and unity. In the 1970s, his music brought the Jamaican people together during times of political conflict. Marley's music introduced people all over the world to Jamaican culture.

Port Royal is a city with six **fortresses**. Its largest one is now known as the Fort Charles Museum. It displays relics such as old weapons used by pirates. The city also has tilted buildings that were damaged in the 1907 earthquake. Visitors can walk on the sloping floors of the old weapon storehouse called Giddy House.

Giddy House was originally built in 1888.

NATURAL WONDERS

Jamaica's Blue and John Crow Mountains National Park is the country's only national park. It includes the Blue Mountains. It is the longest mountain range in Jamaica. Bird-watchers may spot one of 120 bird species, including merlins, falcons, and turkey vultures. Visitors can also tour the Maroon villages or visit a coffee farm.

The Green Grotto Caves on the northern coast feature limestone caves and an underground lake.

The subterranean lake at the Green Grotto Caves is about 39 feet (12 meters) deep.

Visitors can admire the rock formations. They can learn about the caves' history as a hideout for the Taino, Maroons, Spaniards, and enslaved people.

Dunn's River Falls offers cascades of waterfalls nestled in a lush forest. People can climb terraces to reach different waterfalls and enjoy swimming.

Water from the Dunn's River Falls flows directly into the Caribbean Sea.

FACT

Dunn's River Falls is more than 960 feet (293 meters) wide. That's more than the length of three football fields!

BEACHES

Many of Jamaica's beaches can be visited with a short boat ride. Lime Cay is one of Jamaica's several **uninhabited** coral cays. Just off the coast of Port Royal, it offers a beach for relaxing. It is also a popular snorkeling spot.

Seven Mile Beach is well known for its white sand and clear blue waters.

Barracuda

Seven Mile Beach in Negril offers calm and clear blue waters perfect for snorkeling and swimming. Its nearby coral reefs boast colorful tropical fish such as barracuda and angelfish.

Angelfish

Booby Cay is a quiet diving spot. Tropical fish and other marine animals swim along its coral reef.

CHAPTER FOUR

DAILY LIFE

Most Jamaicans live in urban areas. They live in coastal cities such as Kingston. Many live in apartments or small houses called bungalows. Cars and buses provide transportation. Rural residents live in concrete houses or shacks. They often get around on foot or by bus.

Many Jamaicans are in the tourism industry. They may work at hotels or give tours. Some work in offices or shops. Jamaicans also work in the fishing and agriculture industries. They grow coffee bean, banana, and sugarcane crops.

A Jamaican worker sieves coffee beans.

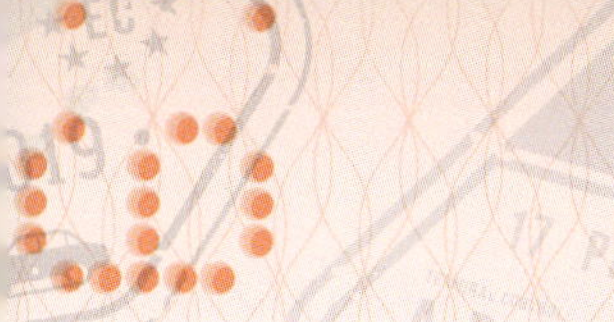

TRADITIONS AND FAMILY

Jamaican families are often close. Many generations may live in one house. Family activities may include going to church. More than half of the Jamaican population is Protestant. A small number of Jamaicans belong to other Christian religions. There are also a small number of Jewish people in Jamaica.

Jamaican clothing mixes British and African styles. Women may wear simple, flowy dresses. Men often wear shirts and shorts. For special occasions, some women wear long, patterned dresses with matching hair bandanas. Men may wear colorful shirts with pants. Schoolchildren often wear uniforms, including button-up shirts and trousers for boys or dresses for girls.

JAMAICAN FOOD

Jamaican food is full of rich flavors. The national dish, ackee and saltfish, is a common breakfast. It features codfish and juicy fruits. Cornmeal porridge and bammy, or flatbreads made from cassava roots, are also eaten. Lunches are usually light.

Dinner is the main meal. Fish escovitch features a fried whole fish topped with cooked vegetables. Many Jamaicans enjoy spiced and grilled chicken or beef called jerk. It is served with fried plantains, rice, or cooked cabbage. Tropical fruits and **traditional** cakes such as sweet and spicy bulla cake are enjoyed for dessert.

Ackee and saltfish

JAMAICAN TOTO CAKE

Toto cake is a popular light coconut cake eaten all over Jamaica. It was first made by enslaved people.

Ingredients

- ½ cup brown sugar
- ½ cup white sugar
- ½ cup softened butter sliced into 1-inch (2.5-centimeter) pieces
- 2 eggs
- 1½ teaspoons vanilla
- 3 teaspoons baking powder
- 3 cups flour
- ¼ teaspoon nutmeg
- 1½ teaspoons cinnamon
- 1 teaspoon salt
- ¼ cup coconut milk
- 1½ cups evaporated milk
- 2 cups grated coconut

Directions

1. Preheat the oven to 375 degrees Fahrenheit (191 degrees Celsius).
2. Grease a large rectangular baking dish with butter.
3. Use an electric mixer to cream the sugar and butter. Add the eggs and vanilla, and mix again for 4 minutes until all ingredients are combined.
4. Sift the baking powder and flour in a small bowl. Add in the nutmeg, cinnamon, and salt.
5. Put the mixer on a medium-speed setting and slowly add the dry ingredients to the butter mixture.
6. Slowly add the coconut milk and evaporated milk.
7. Slowly add the shredded coconut.
8. Once all ingredients are mixed, pour the batter into the baking dish.
9. Bake for 35 minutes, and then let it cool on a rack before serving.

CHAPTER FIVE

HOLIDAYS AND CELEBRATIONS

Many Jamaicans celebrate Christian holidays. Christmas is a festive time. People enjoy music, food, and shopping on Christmas Eve. Families enjoy a big feast together on Christmas Day. Easter is also important to Christians. People visit friends and family. They eat a meal together. It often includes a fruit and spice bun cake.

One week after Easter is the Carnival celebration. Jamaicans celebrate their **heritage** in many events around the island. Dancers in colorful costumes lead concerts and parades. Musicians play rhythmic dance music such as *soca*.

Many bands perform at parades and concerts around the island.

NATIONAL HOLIDAYS

Jamaicans also celebrate national holidays. Labor Day is celebrated in the late spring. Jamaicans clean up their towns and help people in need. Independence Day is celebrated on August 6. Jamaicans enjoy parades, music, dancing, and food in cities across the island.

CHAPTER SIX

SPORTS AND RECREATION

Jamaicans enjoy many sports. Cricket is popular. It is similar to baseball. Cricket players compete in regional games. Jamaicans also enjoying playing and watching soccer. The Jamaican national soccer team has played in World Cup games. Jamaica has many top runners. Many have competed in Olympic Games. Other recreational activities include diving and hiking. Jamaicans of all ages play dominoes at cafés and social events.

USAIN BOLT

Usain Bolt is a world-famous Jamaican sprinter. The eight-time Olympic gold medalist is the fastest runner in world history. He could run more than 33 feet (10 meters) per second!

A cricket match between the Jamaica Tallawahs and the Barbados Tridents during the Hero Caribbean Premier League game.

BULL INNA PEN

Bull Inna Pen is a popular children's game. The larger the group of players, the better.

What You Need:

- six or more people
- a large playing field

What You Do:

1. A group of six or more players holds hands and forms a circle. This is the "pen."
2. One player should stand inside the circle to be the "bull."
3. When the game begins, the bull must try to get out of the pen by breaking out of the circle. The player can try to push out any way.
4. The pen players must keep their hands interlocked and use their bodies to push against the bull. They try to keep the bull inside the pen.
5. If a pen player lets the bull escape, the player must chase the bull down.
6. If the bull is caught right away, the bull goes back inside the circle.
7. If the pen player does not catch the bull, the pen player becomes the bull and a new game begins.

Calypso music originated in Trinidad and Tobago. Street musicians enjoy performing it today.

MUSIC

There is a rich musical history in Jamaica. Reggae is a popular type of music set to drums and guitar. It blends traditional Jamaican musical styles with jazz. Younger Jamaicans enjoy dancehall. It mixes reggae, rap, and disco sounds. Calypso is a gentle rhythmic music played with steel drums.

Jamaica is a country of many cultures blended into one. From its beautiful waters and landscapes to its rhythmic music and tasty meals, there is something for everyone.

GLOSSARY

colonist (KAH-luh-nist)
a person who settles in a new territory that is governed by his or her home country

conquer (KAHNG-kuhr)
to defeat and take control of an enemy

culture (KUHL-chur)
a people's way of life, ideas, art, customs, and traditions

economy (eh-KON-uh-mee)
the way money is made and spent

fortress (FOR-truhs)
large, strong ancient buildings such as castles that kept enemies out

heritage (HAIR-uh-tij)
something received from an ancestor, including objects, ideas, or traditions

immigrant (IH-muh-grunt)
a person who leaves one country and settles in another

Indigenous (in-DI-juh-nuhs)
the original inhabitants of a certain place

traditional (truh-DISH-uh-nuhl)
relating to customs that are handed down

treaty (TREE-tee)
an agreement put in writing

tropical (TRAH-pih-kul)
part of the tropics; the tropics is a hot, rainy region near the equator

uninhabited (un-in-HAB-uh-tud)
not lived in by people

READ MORE

Levit, Joseph. *Track and Field's G.O.A.T.: Usain Bolt, Jackie Joyner-Kersee, and More*. Minneapolis: Lerner Publications, 2022.

Mather, Charis. *A Visit to Jamaica*. Minneapolis: Bearport Publishing, 2023.

Spanier, Kristine. *Jamaica*. Minneapolis: Jump! Inc., 2022.

INTERNET SITES

Britannica Kids: Jamaica
kids.britannica.com/students/article/Jamaica/275127

Kids World Travel Guide: Jamaica
kids-world-travel-guide.com/jamaica-facts.html

National Geographic Kids: Jamaica
kids.nationalgeographic.com/geography/countries/article/jamaica

INDEX

ABOUT THE AUTHOR

Golriz Golkar is the author of more than 70 books for children. Inspired by her work as an elementary school teacher, she loves to write the kinds of books that children are excited to read. Golriz holds a B.A. in American literature and culture from UCLA and a master's degree in education from the Harvard Graduate School of Education. Golriz lives in France with her husband and young daughter, and they all love reading together.

SELECT BOOKS IN THIS SERIES

YOUR PASSPORT TO AUSTRALIA
YOUR PASSPORT TO BRAZIL
YOUR PASSPORT TO CUBA
YOUR PASSPORT TO EGYPT
YOUR PASSPORT TO ENGLAND
YOUR PASSPORT TO GERMANY
YOUR PASSPORT TO JAPAN
YOUR PASSPORT TO MEXICO
YOUR PASSPORT TO PORTUGAL
YOUR PASSPORT TO SAUDI ARABIA